A Life of Prayer & Song

A Life of Prayer & Song

A poetry collection by
Noah Schnaubelt

Cover Illustration: Brianna Schnaubelt
Cover Design & Formatting: Susi Clark of Creative Blueprint Design

ISBN Paperback   979-8-9916196-0-8
ISBN Ebook   979-8-9916196-1-5

To connect, or find more of Noah's heart...
roarandtender.com
Instagram @roarandtender
https://roarandtender.substack.com

For my Mama, the heart she gave me

& ya'll uncountable who've warmed it

& all that has broken it

open

Contents

A Moment to Hold Close to

I wanted to give you a thing beautiful
to keep in your breast pocket,
close to your heart.
Keep deep in your heart
you torch-bearers,
world-watchers,
you fierce lovers,
eyes full of fear and fire,
hands shaking but determined,
soul gasping for answers in the face of darkness,
has there ever been any story but this one?
We ceaseless rebels
planting our feet firm on ever disappearing ground,
but hope and hopeless are just ideas,
poles we swing to
forgetting there is only now,
and in the true moment we are always whole,
hold onto this.
Nothing can ever take you away from yourself.
You can choose to weep
or you can choose to smile,
look death in the face
and laugh all the while,
all this time was only ever borrowed anyway.
Love the one who is afraid
and keep on making wishes.
You can always lift your head and take a breath,
I will love you till the last of mine
and past it,
through every incarnation in and out of time
I'll be here holding embers for your heart.

Days are dark but we
are mighty,
times are hard but we
are stronger,
all these waves are only so long
on the surface of the sea.
Down there in the depths
lies a stillness you can reach,
immovable force of quiet peace.
All of this is only meant to be,
to teach and offer
how to help each other,
and at the bottom there is nothing left
but love
and lover,
you will see.

Rule Number One

Go slowly.
       As you walk.
       As you step.
       In each moment let light
       filter through.
You are so much wild space after all,
       between atoms held together by a love
       of experience,
       you have more room than matter,
       allow it to be filled.
Allow radiance to percolate,
       every small square of your being
       turned over and over again,
Go slowly,
       into this dream
       we call life.
Take the time
       to breathe it in
       to yourself,
       to your bones,
       to that sweet home which is nested
       within your heart
       you are a ghost,
       a spirit,
       a star-whipped traveler.
       You are rider and horse—
       ancient friends,
go slowly.
       In this body,
       learn to move with sensuous reverence.
Go slowly,
       with this mind,
       learn to catch the stories that catch us all inside.

Go slowly,
       through this world,
       learn to see what wonders
       are all around
       you
       have come
       to bear witness
       to a great unveiling.
       To a sea rich with experience,
       to a world so full of beauty
       and might
       that the very air between your molecules
       starts to sing with awe.
Let this be the mortar you make yourself with.
       Let this be the song which resonates
       deep in that cave behind your eyes,
       let this be a knowledge you weave with every breath:
       You were made for appreciation.
       You were born for love.
       You took up shop here on this earth to learn
       to marvel,
go slowly.
       Every step allow yourself
       to take in all that is strewn before you
this world—

       This world,

This World

is a field of treasure
and ripe berries.
Help yourself,
please.

Sunrise

While the air rests with quiet and crisp,
a bird note travels the distance.
Dew hangs as heavy fruit,
becomes golden jewels
in moments
becomes clear again,
infused like we few
up to catch the dawn.

Light plays at this hour.

Feather soft rays drop
like the kiss of a lover
to that sacred spring in the middle of your forehead,
like faerie footfalls,
like the youngest fawn white-spotted
gently bending her head to tender shoots.
The air begins to stir,
every molecule of the world
yawning and stretching their limbs out wide.

Matter grows bigger under light.

This is fact.

With even the smallest hint of warmth
the space between atoms expands.

Will you pause here,
as the rising sun creates you,
can you feel each cell start to dance?

Prayer for the New Day

Great Spirits watch over this wet heart.

      In the morning,
as the sun breaks open onto the world like a shimmer of jewels
turned upside down,
let there be a radiant lightness,
as if each small, red cell coursing through me
was a courier of good news,
a whistling schoolboy,
a bounding puppy.

      In the evening,
when shadows lovingly slip their long fingers around all things
whispering sweetly that the time for rest
has come again,
and the waning moon fills unexpected corners,
let its slender smile be reflected
across all my windows:
Eyes, wide, lucid and absorbing peace.
Palms, open and beaming.
Skin, warm and electric, its own valley
yawning in comfort to this sheet of stars
winking back into being above me.

      In the daytime,
let my work be a parade
of discovery and aid,
let my play be a rush
through my soul, bones and blood,
let my hours dance,
let there be wild songs,
let there be laughter which shakes all parts of me.

And let me build things,
great, mountainous beauties
and tiny, concentrated treasures,
let me inhabit them,
let me give them away.

And in the nighttime,
let my fires roar and crackle.
Let this hearth slowly grow,
let warmth make itself known
like never before.
Let my hours melt and also
the rocks in my shoulders,
like my heart under a smile,
let all drip as these candles
into a shiny, silken pool.
Let times of low light be redemptive,
renewing, and nourishing,
full of strength and wonder.
Let reflection and appreciation blossom,
let my lungs become a still and sturdy bellows.
Let my home become my heart,
a sacred, stable forest glade.
Let soft embers continue to pulse as I sleep peacefully beside them.

The Sky Within

The strength of silence
a blooming quiet
the ground firm.
Muscles poised,
not tense but ready,
a spring with the gentlest fingers trickling away.
The wind of a river,
the loft of a prayer,
a child's balloon and its journey to God.
There is always so much room
to let fear release into,
I pray to feel this open space
more often.
The silence of the dawn
and all its strength
until, like the birds,
I cannot help
but burst
into song.

Invitation

You do not have to worry anymore, my love.

Let this be an invitation.

You do not have to strive nor stretch nor strain so hard.

You do not have to struggle.

Let this be your permission.

Whatever weight you carry,
whatever midnight trouble,
whatever childhood lack still gnawing at your corners.
Whatever frustration fueling a red-alert beneath your smile,
whatever fear,
whatever not-knowing keeps you
moving too fast in hopes of finding, or forgetting.

Let this be a moment you explore,
just for one exhale,
surrender.

This is an invitation to welcome
a new and open-ended future,
one shined in possibility.

You do not have to worry, my love.

Set it down.
Set it all down with a sigh
and know that you are held.

There is a table,
covered in snow-white cloth stretched long as the eye can see
til it's just a thin line glowing deep
into distant mountains.

There is room here to daydream unburdened.

Set all else down.

Whatever ails, torments and troubles rake your mind
or heart or spirit,
set them down, and breathe.
Set them down and share them,
look around,

what can you see?

Here there are
ten thousand other broken pieces,
hearts bereft of blood
and all these unwound watches,
cracked picture glass
and rusted bed springs,
wilted plants
and shards from failed dreams,
paintings half begun
and tarnished crowns
and folded clothes from lovers
long since lost.

Look at this table, up and down,
how far it goes with all of humans' struggles.
Can you see them,
can you feel how we are all the same?

Set it down,
whatever these chains you are holding onto.
There is room here,
share some weight.

You do not have to carry this alone,
you do not have to struggle so.

You do not have to hide,
you do not have to worry,
love,
you do not have to lie.

You do not have to pretend that every moment
is a rare and precious flower.
Some are shit.

You do not have to say all the right things.

You do not have to solve
a single other person's problems.

Just now,
you do not even have to figure out your own.

Just pause.

Let this be an option.

Just stop.
Just rest.
Just breathe.

Take these words,
feel the air, right now, wherever it rests
on any section of your skin.
Feel your toes and fingers,
feel the clothes you chose to walk with
and how they lift and shift with every step,
so subtly with every breath.
Remember the other bodies in this world,
that they have come to share as well,
to cry and laugh and swoon
and how they move
and love,
like you.

Remember the fact:
you are quite literally,
not alone.

Let this be an offering.

There is a world outside
of you
need only to remember.

Pause, and open to it.

You do not have to smile,
you do not have to cry.

You do not owe anything
except what is true inside
and as that changes,
to allow it.
Let it move.
Set it down.
And breathe.

Let this be an invitation.
Come closer.
All of you is welcome.

All of you is welcome here.

The Tender

I am aching to tell you
how deeply I love you.
To crack open a gourd fresh from moist soil,
to shake its seeds around,
to read there in its foundations all
the secrets
to living beautiful,
to growing,
to creation.
I am aching to give you this,
the blessings of simplicity
and magic,
the sweet, sticky guts of it all where we bask,
in warmth and in darkness,
wet seeds waiting to become
green waiting to blossom
ripe vines laden with fruit
towering trees holding the earth
together with the sky
we are
love embodied.
Soft creatures come to discover
and to share,
to blend heaven and earth,
to breathe
and to laugh
and to cry.
We are the nested winds sweeping
through from the mountains,
we are rain collecting in
and down towards the center of all being,

we are the earth heart stone part
coal and ember,
part sun and slumber,
part deep and shadow,
part diamond and thunder.
We are the seeds and the water
the wild and under,
the Care,
in the lick of the tongue
on the head of the young
in the meadow
at birth

We are the tender.

I have been aching to tell you this.
To show you.
To reach deep inside
that shaking heart
and give you all the gold
you hold and cry for,
You, are the tender.
The sweet beloved.
The nectar which you crave beneath the longing,
you are already more beautiful by far,
you are the soul of this whole
mess of a world
SHINING.
No matter what shrouds have encrusted you—
sweet cocoons all of it—
and beneath,
you are the shimmer.

Breathe into this.
Breathe out with this,

the sigh of release of the wave to the beach,
you are the moment
the madness
the magic,
the need,
you are the seed,
sticky and sweet
of all of this.

Holy Artifact

Do You Know How Special You Are?

      That you deserve, more than anything,
to have two hands hold your cheeks with tenderness,
soft suns of eyes shine bright acceptance to your own,
you deserve to have your name softly whispered against your ear
and kisses planted, soft clouds blown
along the arch of your neck.
      You deserve to have two hands wrap
around your waist and pull you   in
to a warm embrace,
your chest rising to meet the breath
of a body that begs to hold you.
      You deserve to be touched
as if your skin was a holy artifact,
each curve and contour treated as treasure,
you deserve to tremble
with pleasure.
      You deserve to be given
piece by piece
to a feeling of ease,
to release through the fierce loving strength of another.
      You deserve to be held,
you deserve to be taken,
in a way that makes every part of your heart
start to open.
You deserve to feel safe.
You deserve to feel high.
      You deserve to feel loved
and you will,

and you will.

And you will.

Let Men Know the Flowers

Let boys be tender.
Let men be soft.
Let this ancient dream of a stone wall
fade,
finally.
There are so many flowers waiting
in the secret and shadowed corners
we are taught never to visit.
Let there be light.
Let there be blossom.
Let the cages built around our hearts
by generations
rust and weaken.
Let us sing like our mothers' prayers for the best of us,
let us cry like our fathers were never allowed.
Let us know ourselves,
all places,
not just the rolling thunder.
Let boys be weak.
Let men be helped.
Let us escape society's perilous directive to be strong and separate,
a martyr alone while our bones weep for holding.
Let us learn instead the weaving,
how hands held in hearts, together,
hold the hope of the good world we all wish
for our children to grow in:
Safety,
and beauty.
Love,
and wonder.
Let men know the flowers,
boys the dancing.
Let our gardens be welcomed,
the quiet blooms as rich
as all the ancient wild.

Fertility

Setting a seed into the soil,
two hands filling the land,
holding them there
as I would over a heartbeat,
putting myself into the ground,
waiting to grow.

Cultivation

Notice, to know this.
Now, is the practice,
always to return.

Begin again.
Become anew.
Befriend attention, welcome
what is here.

The sun's crystal glimmer through the corner of the window
prism takes your skin
blooms with the warmth,
drinks it in.

Trail of an unexpected tear slips through
in the moment when distraction
is given back to breath
and this too, is a gift.
To feel
the slow roll of your rumbling heart
from the soft inside corner of the eye and down;
a second
of presence,
jeweled prayer moist and softening the delicate architecture of
your face.
This sensation.
This phenomenal world and all it offers
to experience.

Notice, to know this.
Cultivate,
create the space to take the pace
of your life as a cup of grace,
sip after sip waiting,
welcome,
endless,
drink your fill.

Hold both hands wide to the glory of sky
that is your heart
that is your mind
that is your time
ripe now,
ready
and open.

Wild Seas

This heart
by now is the color of rust,
buried deep
under wild seas
but,
are not all treasure chests the same?
Scarred, pitted and dented but,
lift the lid and what golden wonder lies beneath?

Inside you will find the magic that you seek.
Lift the lid and watch a thousand petals
rise to the surface,
rose-colored snowstorm in reverse,
a slow-motion flurry of beautiful secrets
released like a hymn
and how these tender notes float,
the hidden song of your deepest nature
at last in harbor under sun.

Every life at some point must begin
to move through the maze built by our own hands;

Our worst and greatest secret,
that these walls we blame the world for
were called into being by our own unruly fears.

We cage ourselves
to protect ourselves
until we have left ourselves
no clear path
to the simplest and most necessary truth:

The decision is yours when to smile.

Wine and Honey

If I am lonely my whole life
I will still
find ways
to sip joy
like sweet nectar squeezed
from a sweet mango every day.
Like kids eating watermelon,
slices as big as our heads
and faces sticky,
hands so sticky,
smiles sticking,
sun warm
warm
warm
down over all around us
warm,
and somersaults over and under and over and under and over again
until
everything
is a spin and a blur of blue and emerald lawn and laughter.
I will still
find ways to let my spirit smile,
I will never despair.
Come universe,
fill this empty cup with wine and honey,
let me shamble around in rags and broken sandals
I will still
toast
everything,
because to be alive is a miracle,
and if I am lonely the whole of it

I am still surrounded by love.
I will still be surrounded by love,
I will pretend until it all becomes real again
and then dance
like only the banjo pickers' fingers know how to dance:
fast,
joyful,
and all through the night.

In Search of Love

There are feathers on the inside of your skin
when you walk
I can hear the wind like brush reeds,
miles stretching out behind you
jet streams,
so much sky soaking in.
You have learned 937 new shapes from the clouds so far,
you have learned the names of three mountains and
their favorite types of rain.
     You have,
from so high in the heavens,
learned that God lives down on the ground,
down there in the details,
in the checkerboard farms
in those goosebump hills
and tributary veins,
in those tiny cartoon creatures all making their way somewhere
     in search of love
you have been walking
upside down in a blue corner,
shaking hands with storms,
getting bit by lightning,
fighting to feel something much clearer
than all this god-damn rain.
     In search of love
you have learned so much about others
but still can't sit still for long enough to feel your own heart
beating
down there in the basement of your chest.

You have given so much of your soul that it's circling the world
like a TikTok trend by now,
have you ever just sat by your own side in the candlelight
and told yourself
"I Love You."

You will.

There are feathers,
fighting to shake themselves free of your bones.
There is God,
fighting to finally be known
in every stone you turn over
there is Love,
937 beautiful shapes of it to play with,
and counting.

Wildfire

There are seeds
crack open to become a tree
only when the heat
of the most destructive fires
tears through.

What furious beatings
these hearts require

to bloom.

Records

I refuse to be pissed off.
I know as a slam poet
I'm supposed to be angry, hurt,
righteously rage-full-of-   shadow,
I'm supposed to decry the ten thousand lies society has sold me, but
I refuse to be the light from a dying star.
And it's not as if I don't have reason.
          I could tell you
of the men who took my body as if it were a paper cup;
cheap soda,
a thing to be crumpled after.
When I moved from a town the size of silence
to a city where the possibility of sexuality was a blossom for the
first time,
18 and never once held hands,
Fresh Meat.
It is still rape even if I did not say no.
It is still rape even if I made the first move.
They should have known
from the way every bone inside of me was trembling,
they should have known when breath failed to escape
caught in my throat like a dead sparrow's song.
They should have known because they were all men
and I was so new.
Paper cup.
A boy to be used.
There are ten thousand questions they could have asked,
placed strong hands soft on shaking shoulders,
uncertainty is not such a difficult book to read.
They should have helped me.

I could tell you
of how my father left when I was two,
planted a specter of loss in such fertile soil.
Could tell you how he left again, slowly
teaching me only how to build walls against trust,
pulling the hopes from my bones to throw as stones
over a cliff into a lonely sea.
		I got trauma,
I could tell you about coming home
to find your roommate overdosed.
About the shredding of a sanctuary,
about holding a man dying in your arms,
about the smell that bubbles through bathwater.
		I could sing you so many songs of sorrow, records
that do not break,
just play
on repeat		play
on repeat		play
on repeat		gray
on repeat		tears
on repeat

		No.

That is not why I am here.

Today
		I will refuse
those siren calls of wounds we all have weathered,
they will no longer commander my vessel.
		I will tell you that haunted
is just another term for holding on,
and I am ready to let go.

Because I have seen the sun rise too.
Because by now I have had lovers
pour colors into my body
that make flowers
sing like the birds.
Because I have a shelf full of vinyl,
and I am learning that the choice is ours
for what we want to play
on repeat   play
on repeat   play
just play.   All day.

    Today
I will tell you of the gardens that my mother grew,
always singing as she placed dinner on the table.
And my stepfather who is still here,
who worked so hard to give us home and healthy.
And I will tell you that bio-dad,
despite his near complete abandonment,
never failed to say he loved me,
and I am ready to remember this,
to allow his song through gates golden with forgiveness.
    I will tell you that the men who take,
are just broken boys themselves,
and while this is no excuse it can allow you to soften.
The echoes of abuse are chains I will no longer use
to keep myself swinging
in darkness.
    I will tell you that death,
it is just another door through which we will wander
wide-eyed, open into wonder.

I will tell you that haunted
is just another term for holding back,
and I am ready to move forward.
To place these records on the shelf,
and to hold instead in my hand the songs
from the smiles of every friend who loves me.
Of which there are many.
      To remember that I have a roof over my head,
a bed to sleep in,
and I have never, not once in my whole life, known hunger.
I am so lucky.
I am so lucky.
WE, are so lucky.
      Today I remind you
of the sparrow's sweet notes as dawn breaks
the horizon into blossom,
and the soft hooting grace of Owl
on even the darkest and most lonely of nights.
      I will tell you that hope, it is like a heartbeat,
learn to breathe and you can always feel it ringing.
Learn to breathe and you'll remember
that in any given moment the choice
it is ours,
to stand up and Sing

a brand new song.

All of You is Welcome Here

The sensation of salt rolling down my cheeks
might be the most familiar
and lately I commit to its wonder.

The greatest gift you can give to your life
is Welcome
to all of it.
To the whole shebang,
to the desperate, the wounded and the tender
as much as any of the sparkle.
Find a home
in the softest positions of your heart
for all its roughest edges,
let them know each other.
Let them all be known.

In this world // to feel // truly is
the most courageous gift you could offer
to your soul or any others.
Let the rains pour
and scream wild with thunder.
All of this is yours
and none of it,
give voice to each divine incarnation
of your feeling,
then watch it empty.
Let the tears roll,
let the laughter bubble without shame,
let the love be as free
as a tumult of birds
taking over an endless sky.

Birthday

The day my mother first set me down into the world
the sky was

       breaking

with thunder.
I have spent so many of my days in rain by now
I wonder
if I can even allow myself to feel fully secure in the sun,

Life of a Poet:

treading this ocean-tide shoreline of light and darkness,
melancholy,
born to be.

I am gifted and challenged to find beauty in even the worst of places,
is it any surprise sometimes that I only feel home when I cry?
But it is a lonely thing,
to curl yourself so deep into a pillow
without knowing why,
The shapes my body would take if I were clouds I'm afraid would

break

the sky

with their weight,

there would be so much thunder.

How many times more must I be born?

There is a wealth of treasure I know must glow around every corner;
take me home,
somewhere as I learn to run,
there is a path lit with ten thousand lanterns,
may I never be dressed in such a storm-front of questions again.

Heavy Blossoms

Depression
is thick tar
muddy air
muffled sounds
synapses firing into space
like shotguns into the sky on a TV on mute.
There is so much energy buckling
and not connecting,
so much electricity running into rubber,
there is just so much fucking sadness.

Am I a conduit to the weight of the world I sometimes wonder?
Am I still just working off all the pain I couldn't as a kid?
Am I a big, gay thirty-something mess lost and searching
for meaning?
Am I just overwhelmed perhaps,
am I just sometimes chemically imbalanced,
am I just cursed,
am I just given a strange blessing to feel so god-damned deeply?

There is no answer I think.

There is just an ocean
which swells
and pours out through my head.
How can I contain so much, I wonder?
I do not understand.

Depression
is a turtle on its back in a mud-hole
at night
with no stars,
slow limbs waving
and a tiger circling,

taunting,
and growling low.
It is a sense of senselessness,
of feelings
blocked,
a weight that hangs heavy and rocks
slowly,
a ten thousand pound pendulum suspended from a gray sky and I
am trying to let myself feel such things,
instead of running away running
as I have my whole life;
what is this darkness which is a part of me?

Depression is a fear
that when I start crying
I may never stop.
And it's not a hurdle I can hop over,
it's not some wall I can climb over,
I can't ninja this shit,
this buzzing
this fog
this top-heavy heat that blankets my thoughts.
There is a hole
to an ocean
which comes through,
and it's all I can do to hold on against a tide
I do not understand.

Maybe I can't.

Like the moon and her dance,
like the seasons,
like death and his thieving,
maybe I'll never be able to know why.
I have tried
and I have puzzled

and I have tried
and sometimes I just want to cry
and it scares me.
The same black beast which throttled
both a grandmother and an aunt
has been circling as far back as I remember
and he is heavy in my head,
and I am tired.

And I have learned how to live
remarkably well, considering the claw scars in my shoulders.
I have learned how to laugh,
how to pretend,
and to *know*
that pretending becomes reality again
and right now,
I am tired.

I have learned that I am mighty,
loved,
supported.
That I can get along through anything,
that even when this thread is cutting off my breath
I can still swim on and tread
oceans
and right now
I am tired.

I am learning that Depression
is just a part of my life.
And always will be.
And I am strong.
And right now,
I am tired.

Mine

In this strange moon world
teach me a new song;

some particular steps of a secret;

teach me the dance of copper,
gold,
and silver
as they weave through the cave wall,

how to become beautiful
and precious

in the dark.

Emptying out a Heart

        In a pile
we have silver screws and dried rose petals,
boxes swollen with pictures,
we have an ear that is well worn in from listening,
we have so many black tears.
Deeper
we have sailboats,
shiny rings.
        Emptying out a heart—
turning it upside down and shaking;
clicking bugs drop out,
train-chimney-stack smoke,
tawny wheat fields,
smiles from mom,
several cogs,
leaf after leaf after leaf:
some wet muck some
star-fire glow some
crunchy brown, others still green
as praying mantis.
        Emptying out a heart—
reaching in with gloved hands
and pulling up
anchors,
huge chains,
empty picture frames,
lion paws
and the flip of a kitten's tail,
we find
a kid on the floor hands curled around
knees curled up head down between them.

Deeper,
we find music notes.
Whale songs.
Bursts of gold light,
little flares peppering a blank space,
we find light-years of darkness,
a sense of too much gravity.
      Emptying out a heart—
all the skulls still rattling inside each chamber;
doorknobs
and keys and combination locks
dropping through it
we have weathered books,
looks frozen and rusted aimed at what could not be:
old crushes
half dreams
stunted limbs.
Deeper:
blankets,
dark oceans,
salted grounds,
empty pages,
thousands and thousands and thousands
of poems.
      Emptying out a heart
somehow,
making space for something bigger.

Exit Sign

I write poetry because
as they say
no one understands.
The weight of the world settles differently on everybody's shoulders.
Sometimes when I wake up
my room has been filled with water,
the wet pages of the books I love
float by me upside-down
like dead things,
window light looks different filtered through an ocean,
all ships underneath are merely skeletons
or phantoms.
Have you ever been held upside down in a corner?
I never knew sound could make it so hard to breathe,
the racing drum of my heart
in a battle with these lungs
I am in civil war,
and like a displaced villager unable to know
the forces tearing me apart;
victim of my own self-doubt and disbelief
and *will*
does not necessarily equal strength,
just because I always move forward
does not mean I can pull myself up
and the nights are always colder when you're struggling.
I write poetry because often it is the only exit sign
still lit,
but sometimes it's in a crowded amphitheater
and I am so full of panic squeezing life into a single line.
I write poetry because it is the one thing I am consistently good at
besides desperation.

Because my hands don't reach far enough to rub my own shoulders.
Because a vacuum and a whirlwind amount to the same thing.
Because there is nowhere else to fit this ocean.
Because some part of me still wonders if it's possible
to trade something broken
for something whole.

Sunlight Still Fills a Canyon

Let me remain open
even as I wander this gauntlet
let some small magic guide my hand.
Let every seemingly blind step
still be towards a place of wonder,
let me know
there is even greater joy to follow.
Let life grow besieged by beauty
through this rift,
this canyon
as I drift,
in this canoe
amidst the west blue ocean,
under darker skies,
let me know it is only to find new islands,
ones laden with treasure.
Let the weights I feel bearing down
be met with equal pleasure
soon enough,
let me catch glimpses
of mythic creatures out the corner of my eye.
In every shadow
let this grief be strong
and then be done,
a dawn breaking,
leaving a bounty of space in its place
please,
let this darkness still birth meaning
I can't see now
but even so,
will bring me wisdom.

An Old Home

There is a grief which sits within me.

At most times just a hint, faint and subtle
like a siren in the city's distance,
small tell-tale sign that not all
is quite right
and yet,
but,
the sun still shines.
The lights operate,
the doors open and close,
birds take to the sky.
I must go on,
for the sake of all the life left in me,
and pay little heed to the blotch of smoke
on the horizon.

At other times most
of my energy is wasted
as dark water floods the streets.
A thousand thousand voices scream from rooftops,
I am paralyzed to hear or help them all.

There is a grief which sits heavy behind
most of the scenes that are made in my mind,
I bleed before I can ever realize their illusion.
This peculiar weight of uncertain things,
a ceaseless accosting roil of clouds
that shutters any progress I might gain
beyond 'okay'.

I feel sometimes

as if long ago
a great promise was made in my bones
and then broken.
I'll be trying to patch holes forever
from places I was too young to understand
and am now too old to remember.

There is a grief composed like granite
of a hundred different horrors

feardoubtguiltshame
confusionlossangerself
hatredworrysorrow
lonelinessdeprecation
embarassmentinferiority
powerlessisolation
terrifiedthreatened
guardeddeniedunknown
judgmentanxiety
afraidandalone

There is a body, intangible,
and yet so thoroughly attached
to every ounce of me,
that was built brick by broken brick
until it housed and tainted all of me.
Before I learned to breathe I was already
being bested by the trials of this world.

There is a long grief
which has made me its old home.

On good days I still carry myself like a puppet in a daze,
sticking close to bright windows,
avoiding dark corners,
choosing the world outside and to turn
a blind eye to the rest
because I don't know how to face
what I don't know how to know.

And on bad days there is no hope.
The sun never rises.
Outside the windows in the blue and dark
is a parade of the same
city on fire,
submerged.

Into Great Sky

Holding the heart open
until it beats with joy again;

discovering truth
defining magic
defying gravity,

all my songs for feathers.

Lassos

There are broken tree limbs,
children's shoes tangled in roots
and forgotten.
There are angry seas—
violent seas—
and all manner of bedtime legends
useless for truly teaching how to cross them.
There are footprints in the underside of thunderclouds
as if the hero traveled upside down to try and stop the storm.
The rain still came.
The rain still comes.
There is the struggle of past lives coinciding with real time troubles.
There are nooses woven out of kites' strings,
lassos twisted with dark rings,
fairies caught by the left heal
wings fluttering faintly
and dreams,
long ago undelivered, yet unable to die.

Depression

Open my hands out to grace,
beg for a flower,
bow my head to the thunder
of silence
which is surrounding
so thick I am afraid of drowning.

I pray for a better understanding
of the significance
of separation
from the Source.

I pray to be more okay
here,
folded into this cardboard box,
dusty and unsure
where I am being sent to.
I am willing
to *be* here,
heavy in this body,
amongst the shadows as often
as the light which has created them.
I *am* here,
willing some small miracles to show
when I am filled with less
illumination.
I am scared
of where my life will turn,
of how to take it back.

I am saddened
for no reason I can divine in the moment,
I am well versed
in sudden heat.
I am asking
not to be taken out of this,
but just for understanding.

How do I treat myself with what is present,
how do I trust that this is where I need to be,
how do I relax with sorrows,
how do I feel my way around
when I am feeling down,
how do I go into darkness while still cultivating ease?

I hold my arms wide,
hands open to grace.
I am *here*,
In this body,
a floating petal,
a willing seed.

Brimming

Adj: To be so full, on the point of spilling over...

The soft orbs of your eyes
are so shined with wet
as if all mountain lakes are rushing to come through them.
You are so close to tears my dear
and, you are So Damn Beautiful,
if you will only believe me when I tell you:
Every drop you contain about to drain in two delicate streams
down your cheek
is each one a more perfect hole in the making
for sweet sunshine to replace them.

You will be overrun,
I promise,
with so much joy your body
will not be able to stop humming.

You will be taken over,
crystal glaciers reflecting azure spaces.
You will be such a radiant sky
all the birds in all the world with all their wings thrumming
will take flight
inside
your heart
will be given the softest bed of feathers to rest in;
tucked under the breast of a mother sparrow
in first morning light,
all your narrow corners will have soft chimes
sparkling around them.

You will be engulfed.
You will be the carved chamber inside a laughing bell,
so resonant with sound
the rest of us can do nothing but look up and smile.
You will be the wide, round disc of a high, full moon
and every kiss of every lover beneath her.

You will be overwhelmed my dear,
I promise,
with enough beauty to make the breath catch in your throat
and swell
until your exhale is a shooting star,
every wish worth having taking root inside your chest.

You will be made new again.

You will be made new.

So cry, my love,
right now,
hold back nothing.
Let your oceans spill over.
Sob and sigh,
release,
lay down into this tide and choke
knowing it is only passing through you.
The wildest of storms still cleans,
leaves all this room to fill.
Let go what belongs now only to the past
and you will be rebuilt,
I promise,
ten thousand times greater,
every small square of your being spun
like a clay cup in a potter's warm hands.

You will be glowing,
so soon,
set to rest in a warmth sweeter
than you ever knew,
soaking in so much light and laughter,
all but overflowing with love
my friend,

you will be brimming.

A Soul Lost Too Soon

I wish I could carry you through all this.

To a place where the space his death creates
is but a small warren surrounded by wildflowers.

I wish my arms could reach the distance
between stars and feathers,
between hearts and thoughts of whether
you
could have changed the channel
of his river's rushing course.

I am placing the darkness in ten thousand rivers
with ten thousand currents in hopes
that a destination where the water pools
like Sunday afternoon and clarity
will be reached so swiftly.

I wish that I could pluck out answers
as easily as berries off the bush
and give you solace.

I am finding the sweetest summer rains
to wash your face
when you are crying.

I am setting sparrows in your heart
so all your hurt may fly someday.

I am collecting wild rocks to build a tower with,
ten thousand miles high,
so that the moon herself takes notice
and stays full for months,

her gentle light guiding your shadows into tides
full enough to hold them all
and carry the pain away.

I wish I could sit there
weeping willow by your side,
offer you tea,
shade you with my branches,
let every star peeking through
become a candle in the window
burning softly,
ever shining against the injustice
of all such tragedies.

I am feeding all his pictures to the wind
so that she'll carry you in dreams
to streams where hands and hearts will touch again.

I am swinging my fists in the face of such loss,
there is no reason

there is no reason

There Is No Fucking Reason sometimes
for the blade that carves our lives into pieces of time
with far too little light,
I am so sorry this dark thundercloud
has broken down your doors and filled the house.

I am planting trees in all your corners
so there will be ever more air to breathe
as time goes by.

I am singing to you
like he has sung,
like he is singing now:
in every sunrise birdsong dewdrop shining,
in every river's babble,
in every fire's crackle,
in every moment of silence—
he is strumming that guitar
and singing love.

I am putting a kitten into your lap
and a soft puppy by your side
and a bowl of ice cream
and a storybook
and that picture I think he's five in
and naked and eating watermelon as big as his face.

I am feeding you every simple joy
I can dream up to distract you.

I wish I could wind your heart up like clockwork
to ensure you'd be alright.
I'll stop by once every day to do so,
to keep you running at full speed,
I'll never forget, not even once,
I swear it.

I wish I could catch all of these arrows for you,
shield you from the heavy stones,
cast my body over the flames,
drink in all the darkness,
feel the suffering ten times stronger in my own heart
so that your burden would be less.

I am carving all of these icebergs into roses
and lotus blossoms for you,
setting them adrift
with a gentle kick under the full moon
so that soon
your shores will be deluged by beauty.

I am putting all four limbs
to the ground
and running head down yowling
to raise the packs and herds and prides
and all the creatures will gather,
howl, roar and cry
once every year to remember
a soul lost too soon.

I am reshaping a mountain range
into his name
so every creature flying
whether wing or in a plane
will look down and remember
a soul lost too soon.

I am tearing walls apart,
crumbling rooftops,
blowing trees down,
opening caves up to the sky,
I am writing his name across the heavens
using every single star
so that it burns ten thousand miles wide
and brighter than the sun in daylight,
and every creature will look up and remember
a soul lost too soon.

I am holding all your hands together
as we place Jessiah into a canoe,
stand in the sand
and sail him over the flat ocean edge of the world.
And we will smile
and cry together,
watching as the universe itself welcomes him home,

this beautiful soul lost too soon.

Afterlife

In the truth of death remember how to live,
this time it is not borrowed but is given.
This world a chest of treasure thrown wide open,
each breath a sacred song if you will listen.

When you pause and let the sky become your life,
whether shine or thunder all imparts a lesson.
Through grace of pure acceptance, transformation,
each moment, you will learn, can be a blessing.

You could mourn the seconds dropping—leaves on fire,
or know them all as stars shoot 'cross the night.
There is comfort to be found instead of grasping,
all things pass and in so doing cast their light.

So Go,
move through this world and every note she offers,
keep your heart two palms held open, welcome all.
When it breaks allow the pieces wings and listen,
when it sings your smiles shared will crumble walls.

So Go,
each moment that you can love, watch them shimmer.
Give your thanks then find your breath and let it fly.
Be courageous and be patient when you stumble,
may each lesson be a blessing till you die.

This time it is not borrowed, but is given,
may each lesson and each blessing ease your life.

Shatter

Let it be a continual breaking,

until even the dust is reduced to indeterminate atoms and
what that remains:

uncountable pieces of light.

Just for You

I am lighting this candle
and placing it gently into your heart.
When life is ever at its darkest,
there is love burning for you.
There are the tears of all great poets emptying beside you,
there is welcome space
for so many stars to bloom.
There are railroad tracks lifting
and curving into the sky,
there is a glory of sparrows
making curious shapes
like children's clouds
and singing as you search to find your pathways.
I am not praying for you,
I am decreeing,
with all the power of God
and her firecracker
of a universal jumpstart behind me,
that Things Are Going To Be O-K.
and by things

> I mean dreams.
> And desires.
> And fears
> and searching
> and tears
> and hurting
> and wishing
> and years
> and waiting

and yearning
and hoping
and fighting
and moments

where the wind is whipping his hardest to knock you off the cliff,
it is all going to be ok.
Whether you fall or fly or climb
or hike back down
you *will* reach the sea,
and ten thousand candles in little boats will float
into your heart.

Smash Funk

Today is a bit more of a click rattle shiver
trying to carve butterflies out of cinderblocks
instead of smashing car windows
day after day
the heat inside my palms
burning circles
edge of an eclipsed sun
the tremble of lungs as a tree falls
screaming
today

is a puzzle box opened up under water
so many cardboard flashes of color in sunlight in a dizzying swirl
today is a first-rate cutthroat hack-job
a stiff gulp of blood and salt
a bitter before-taste tainting
whatever follows down the path
is an obstacle course and a blindfold
a repeat offending rear-ender
a stolt-judder grab-bag
a pissed-off cartoon ape
today

is a lesson in frustration
in the inevitability of pendulums
in breathing over and over and again over just
to stay still
today

is a couch-fort cower day
a where the fuck is dad day

a monsters scratching at the front door day
today is for throwing nails at cold lumber
for kicking reflections in a puddle
hiking to the top of a mountain and flipping off the stars
today

is blind rage and black tar
a sinuous furnace
one eye and sharp steel
today is a smash funk
a backlit kickdrop
a fright flight knife fight
a punching bag wrapped in wire
makeshift battery and a butcher knife to stab in it
today

is a wannabe
is an ought to be meant
not to be
today is a ship sailing straight
into a big damn cliff
today is a hangnail
today is the flip switch shift of a fox tail
wicked jester's grin
the trickster getting your goat
leaving nothing but the entrails
today

is a fucked up witches brew
a calamitous comedy
a sharp note in a tin room
today is a bad echo
a fast trip flop
in slow motion capture
today

is a crumbling windmill
castle collapsing
hard ocean pounding with runaway rocks
a shoreline held captive
to the screeching flocks.

Morning Gray

A car slides like a ghost through its reflection
in the window down the hill from me.

In a cold, gray and beautiful sunrise I try to remember
what it's like to feel something.

Over my head a haven of grasping branches
sets forth three birds,
I watch the undulation of their thin lines in unison
disappearing through the distant wall of fog.

So many clouds have come to share the riches of the sun
it seems there is none left for the rest of us
save a solo, piercing beam,
this glowing shine the size of a solitary ship,
splashing onto the bay almost as far away as the eye can wander.

How the water glitters.

I have been wishing all morning I had
some new words to say about depression.

Maybe if I'm as fortunate as I can't remember right now,
I'll find their peculiar sound real soon.

The days and the nights will never cease their revolutions,
each season and the waving tides demand their rightful turns.

Here in the middle the best, I think, that we might hope for
is appreciation,

what direction towards even the smallest wonder of a moment
can we choose?

Be Gentle

There is no shame in feeling strange,
there is no blame to be placed on inaction.
Fear is a most powerful force
and wherever you have before
been frozen,

know that you were learning still.

Offer love to all iterations of your self
which remain contained within.
Be gentle with your precious heart,

we heal in our own time.

Hive

Mostly I find a crowd of bees on the inside of me.
Once in a while a sparrow sings,
                    a small star winks,
                    an ocean waves friendly
but mostly heavy,
my bees are made out of lead,
they stay-stick-stutter in the same
                                   graywashed places.
I've sung your name more times than I have spoken it
and still heard not even an echo.
We're all just a stones throw from any number of new directions
but I remember your arms and how difficult it was to lift them.
You were a giant and I made of paper straws,
I remember your heartbeats and sifting myself through them,
the spaces we can't see are the deepest we squeeze ourselves
inside of
and what exactly qualifies as necessary loss?

I know that I have found myself

smaller   bigger
               at the
best   worst
               of times

I've transformed into far more pieces
than one can keep track of,
a ravel of wings and a clutter of stings
and always this lure of honey
and always this wind and its cold demand for shaking.

In the outside of outside of me somewhere
there is space to gather,
     but the outside of inside me
so much scattered,
          bodies tumble
and the buzzing grows louder,
            I can't tell what direction to fly towards.
I am ghost, memory and clouded vision
struggling to reach the tops of trees
and a calm meadow someways beyond them.
     In the inside of inside of me
when the swarm mellows
I know there are steady candles,
I've glimpsed them
and trails of footprints to forgive,
but I am stone after stone dropped through the hive
and I don't know how to keep calm in the storm.
     Somewhere inside outside of me
a star winks,
a sparrow sings,
and an ocean carries islands dripping with nectar,
long toppled,
but humming still, to be rightly turned over.

Hope

There is so much sometimes
I feel as if I am made of nothing else.
But hope is not always easy,
a chain made of light still keeps you bound
and weightless sounds the same as empty right about now.
I am not crying though I wish I was
letting out again those sweet silver prayers to God.
I am not desperate but I am wishing,
I don't know how to live without it,
        Hope.
Sometimes this
is a songbird whistling from a tree top
the whole day shiny and open.
Sometimes this is a hungry wolf
gnawing on an old bone.
Sometimes this is a lifeline,
sometimes a noose we can't help but slip our whole self into.
        Sometimes this is an ellipses,
three dots staring into darkness,
an old photograph,
a candle
and a prayer.
Sometimes
this is a song that puts your heart
in a blossom
on a cloud puff
curled around a wing rising
into the oceanic sky.

Sometimes
this is the last plank of an old ship
in a merciless sea.
Sometimes hope, it is a monster,
a teasing hand held out
and a gauntleted fist bearing down,
it will all but drown you,
keep you prisoner in its corner
and smile to watch you creep along to find a place to breathe.
And sometimes
hope will shine you,
will take every rough and held back dreaming
and let them soften with a breath
and a slow unwinding.
Like a green leaf floating down a stream,
you will see
direction vary but flow is always present
and this journey ever towards unknown is,
beneath all these great trees,
still vibrantly ensconced in beauty.
And hope,
it is a creature
who will live always inside of you
and never,
never once stop singing.

A Mansion of Sorrow

I remember
ten thousand ways of missing
something I never knew
in the first place.
Home
is where the heart is they say
but growing up gay
puts your heart in the hardest place
The Closet—
is just a front door
to a whole mansion of sorrow.
There are places I still fear
the sun could not find its way inside;
when I wake up first thing
with my jaw a masterpiece of tension
and my hands ache from squeezing,
I wonder when that little boy first started clenching
and how far down I still need love to shine?
Days like these I start to cry,
not for no reason,
but because my heart was freezing
before I could ever share a thing.
There are mountains
made out of monsters that don't even matter anymore,
but the shadow they cast is a labyrinth I fear
I may never walk out of completely.
Home
is something I've had to slap together piece by piece
and I never really learned how to use a hammer;
sometimes when the walls start to shake
I wonder if this blood
will ever truly know its place.

I Love You Keep Going

You are almost there.

Put your head down into this wind,
smile that secret smile,
put one foot in front of the other
and keep moving.
This storm is vast,
these droplets cold,
the view obscured,
but just around the corner is a cave
and a fire
and whole swarm of magic,

you are almost there.

Know even as your arms feel heavy with rain
that I am cheering you on
and rattling stars around the space inside your chest,
there is nothing but love for you to fall into
you are so much more
than ok.

There is wonder wished into this world
just for you,
it waits to press itself through your skin
like a puppy burrowing for warmth into your arms,
there is nothing but love streaming your direction.

Take heart,
stay connected to this heart,
know
that you are always
connected to this heart.

Know that it is beating loud for you to follow
through the darkness
and you will
and you are,
and even as every sense seems to sputter
like a candle struck by thunderstorm,
know this,

you are almost there.

The Color of Truth

I wear my heart on my sleeve and it bleeds a lot,
blood stains on all my windows
I've been trying to get outside   myself.
Said goodbye last night to my love in new way,
woke up this morning and coughed out a thundercloud.
Sometimes the sound in my mind goes so fast
it makes my blood boil,
it's all vibrations anyway and right now
we're just on different wavelengths.
Can't give change to the homeless on the street
I'm still trying to find enough for myself,
tear off strips of my soul though and hand em out
like I'm feeding the damned
every day.
If my body was a book I'd be in every free-box begging to be
read,
somebody teach me how to translate all these bird cries,
I think they're laughing at me
every morning
I just try to find space in a world which cares
so much about what doesn't matter,
submerged in a bathtub full of milk and blood
I can't reach any of my senses.
Some of my earliest memories
are of loneliness,
I don't know if I've ever felt as if anything is possible.
Gratitude is a saving grace and I've been trying
to learn to live inside of it,
but so often just feel like I'm struggling with
the same old shit.

I carry a second body stuck to every cell by a shadow,
he's a man made out of everything that I can't understand quite yet.
I spend my days fighting to love
and my dreams wishing for a hug big enough to break me
open,
I've been hopin'
somehow for a little bit of transformation,
to touch my fingers to this cold glass box
and see the world like Picasso outside of it,
but I'm also afraid of it,
afraid I'll never fit,
afraid I'm only this
mind of broken lines and rhymes that don't find nothing to do
except repeat themselves except
repeat themselves
accept,
repeat.
I've cried more times than God could count
about what I can't comprehend.
I feel
like the world wants us all to be beautiful
but maybe what that means will always be a mystery.
I know
that every hand must hold a storm inside of it
and try to say that when it rains it's still a nice day.
Carry a box under my arms with every color made from sunrise,
got my face painted last week and she gave me a panda.
When the world is black and white it's easy to find direction,
but under shades of gray these street signs all begin to blur.
I go walking through downpour sometimes with no clothes on,
get so tired of always being protected.
Built battle armor by the time I could speak
and then lost myself inside of it,
an iron suit in the closet is no place for a child to grow in.

I fear sometimes that though I've broken out
I'll never escape the shape of it,
afraid I've formed to fit.
Guess that's why I try to care so much now,
try to show so much now,
try to grow and touch more than enough now,
breaking out ten times ten thousand fold I just
want to play with love in every moment
and even the sidewalk sings if you'll listen
with the drumbeat of your footsteps.
I feel
like a man made solely out of mud sometimes,
trying so hard to be a real boy,
to bake in the sunshine
walk through the fire,
toughen up this skin even as I transform to something beautiful,
a vessel built out of butterfly dreams.
There's a boy I gave my heart to
at the same time I was being born,
I don't really want it back now
but I think I need to,
we've been taking turns destroying each other
for longer than I care to admit so
I just bro

       ke
it
off.

And I'm feeling like shit.
Like I'm just gonna miss,
cutting off limbs to find balance,
like I'm waving goodbye to my soulmate.
There's so much growth we've each got to reach I guess
but sometimes I wish I could just speak Moon,

so I could understand these tides completely.
There's a mystery built into even the most mundane of moments
and a magic that only the hardest of pains can show us
and all I can do now
is pray.
Put my palms to the ground
let the blood drip down
and try to feel light
as I try to feel life
as I shiver and cry
will I heal and grow wise
what's next for these eyes
I am afraid.
And excited.
And lonely.
This heart.
This heart,
this heart is too big for this body,
too much for this soul
so I've sewn it on a leash to my sleeve
and I'm slinging it around like a yo-yo,
let it sleep.
Make it spin.
Learn new tricks go for walks Eiffel Tower
build a tower climb to the top
bury my bones in the stars,
throw myself to that wide net of wishes
and I will wait,
where your eyes sunset glow,
cradled there in the basin of the big dipper
bruised and exposed and bleeding.
And I will work,
washing each one of these windows clean
and beating my chest to the thunder under a mountainous sky

until all that is left
is a furor of beauty.
And the shattering from necessity
will become the wings of illumination.
And my sleeves will dry,
dyed the color of truth,
and maybe,
maybe
there will be peace.

Attachment

I shall want as long as I live.
I know this
and will myself regardless,
to let go—

They say it's the way,
to love the falling leaf
and the lean, curved fingers left
of the branches;
how they hold the sky when barren,
how they curl around the moon.

Sometimes I forgive myself for hoping—
it's a child's world after all.
It's a realm of circles, cycles and spinning,
it's revolutions,
how the innumerable forces of the grass
push away the winter's wall come springtime,
their blades thrust past the mass
of cold, unburdened earth at last,
at last.

How to Deal With Depression:
Vol. Whatever

1)   Know that you will be ok.

2)   Fuck everything.

19)   You must be strong in simple ways.

16)   Order will leave you.
Don't try to force it.
Roll where you are taken,
the tides have become you for a time.

17)   Focus will leave you.
You'll have to learn to be okay
with sliding around,
spacing out,
losing track
even more than normal.
But half-finished thoughts are still
a point on a map,
trust.

7)   Remember,
you are truly more fortunate than you feel right now.

6)   Deep Breaths.
Wisdom as old as time has got to be worth something.
When you can't run, walk.
When you can't walk, crawl.
When you can't crawl, breathe.
This is your body's point of entry to life,
this is your soul's point of entry to your body.

Breath
is a bridge,
move out on it.
When all else is in a tumble
you can still declare one tiny moment
at a time
to be yours.
Start over,
be simple:
Inhale.
Exhale.
Breathe.

13) Remember to drink water,
remember to eat.
Give your body these most basic of necessities.

3) Fuck everything else.
The mantle of life outweighs us all at points,
let it go.
Be humbled,
be slow.

11) Are you sad? Be sad.
Are you afraid? Be afraid.
Are you angry? Be angry.
Depression is disconnection,
its poisons are profound,
but present somewhere there is truth,
lean into this.
Let the weight press you, deep
rest,
feel.
Allow yourself to feel what lies beneath
and you will start to heal.

There's energy needing to move through you
and it is painful but important.
No one can hold back the tide for long.

5) Chocolate.

15) Chocolate.

10) Chocolate.
Bath.
Blanket and a nap.
Buy yourself some flowers.
Take a short walk.
Zone out to a favorite movie.
Give yourself small kindnesses
repeatedly.
You are feeling small right now,
respond in kind.
How would you help a child who is feeling awful?

You are that child,
offer yourself the same tender love.

4) Reach out.
You are more loved than you will ever know.
You don't have to carry this alone.
Family,
a friend,
a stranger on a lifeline,
there is *always* someone who will help you
share such weight.
You might, but don't have to understand.
You might, but don't have to explain.
Just tell someone you're not feeling OK
and let yourself be hugged,
let yourself be loved.

8)   Go Outside.
        Park
        Woods
        Mountains
        Ocean
        Sky,
        make yourself go outside.
        There is so much room in this world,
        open, waiting beauty,
        you will feel lighter.

18)   Nothing has been taken from you
        but it has been taken over.
        You cannot fight what you feel,
        as painful as it is your darkness
        must be given harbor
        in order for it to heal.
        Let these broken ships drop anchor,
        there's treasure they still hold,
        allow yourself to deal,
        there's work that must be done
        instead of taking cover.

9)   Music
        is the embodiment of the heart,
        a vehicle for the soul,
        a boundless ocean big enough to hold you.
        Do not go without it.

12)   Cry.
        Don't be afraid to.
        This is how darkness is washed through the spirit
        and out of the body.
        This is you
        becoming one

with the depths
until there is no other option but evacuation.
Allow yourself to drown if need be,
and a little while later
you will feel lighter.

14)   Be patient. With the world. With yourself.

20)   "It is always darkest before the dawn."
        "This too, shall pass."
        There are truths which are too ancient to be cliché.
        Have faith in this if nothing else.
        Remember you have been here before,
        have come out all right,
        have been the opposite:
        bursting with light.

        Remember.

        Start over at number one.

        As often as you need.

Grace

I gather my shame and I
let
     it
          go
into the arms of deepest love.

I could continue these patterns my entire life,
change nothing,
and still be worthy
of extraordinary grace.
I am young still,
unguided,
helpless hopeless lost
in many parts of this tender, broken and
beautiful being.

It is no wonder these desperate tendencies,
grown with no outside wisdom
or hands to help me,
still take over.

I forgive myself for everything I have ever felt I have done wrong.

Including,
including the dozen times or more each day
I still betray
the lessons I have so far gathered.

There are needs unmet which choke me still,
which broke me,
which pull the hope from me,
which rope me into madness
despite my greatest of intentions.

I am a small man and
a large, unlearned child.

I promise
to try my best always
to be softer and more loving
as I tread trembling through trails
where wisdom's rarely granted.
I pray for the space and the unfolding I've been begging for,
I release shame
into the warmest of embraces,

there is absolutely nothing wrong with me.

I'll say it as often as I can remember
until I'm able to know it as the truth.
I do. I do. I do.

Partners

The universe prays for you to dance
just as much as you pray for the wisdom
to recognize the steps.

A Pact

Make every act
a declaration
of unashamed Self Love.

With all you do.
With every step,
with every expansion of those lungs inside your chest,
with every sip of water,
lips lightly pressed to the rim of a cool glass.
With every twist-click-unlatch of a doorknob,
every sideways glance caught on your own reflection,
every time you set your bones down to rest
on a chair, couch, floor, or the bed.
With every shoelace tied and untangled,
with every shirt shrugged into,
with all that you do,
bring countenance of love.

And know that you are worthy.
That you are a wise and tender creature.
Know that the Sun
and the Moon
both smile
to see how their light
plays on your face
every time.
Know that you are a special kind of magic.
However wounded and weathered,
remember that for every sorrow and shame,
for every guilt and anger,
for every secret and shadow,
you
are deserving in equal measure
a wild and joyous loft,

a parade
of fearless love.

Know this.

Know this.

Know it, and be soft
with yourself.
Sigh often.
Touch your fingertips to your own heart featherlight
and whisper
"I am the sweetest thing."

Because You Are
the sweetest thing.

My greatest wish is that you will remember this:
with every fork lifted to your face you are feeding God.

And through every single moment,
from the first fluttering
of your eyelashes back to consciousness in the morning
until you rest your head at long last in the wee hours,
I hope you move remembering
that love
from ten thousand golden dreamers always moves with you.

Allow yourself to believe.

You. Are. Loved.

You. Are. Love.

I

love

you.

Inventory

My brain will give you an itemized list
of every reason not even the sun should love me.
It will add footnotes, addendums and translations
into all manner of languages culled
from the dark void of space
it will photocopy ten thousand pages to scatter as blizzard,
a flock of seagulls drowning out the sky,
picking at the dead.

My heart will be a pomegranate
split
down the center and fallen open,
two raving halves:
       one a nest of the finest jewels, unmarred and shining.
Their translucent, rich cluster of unparalleled sweetness,
a potency of seeds
bare, ripe and willing.
       The other is a wilted maze in thick and calloused shell,
browned fruit long tilted towards decay.
A plethora of wonderment, dreams, and desires left to bitter,
packed so tight together in their hurts and disappointment
no chance exists to avoid the rot which creeps its way.

My lungs...
They've learned a lot,
try to be an anchor
weightless and yet rooted;
launchpad, journey and destination.
They billow, I sail.
They contract, and I still.
When I remember, when I am able,

there is home in their moment.
Breath becomes bridge to presence
welcoming
any, all, and everything.
Soft and compassionate allowance,
there is grace in that truth of the now.

My time is a Rorschach,
hurricane and island.
It is   un   fold   in g
origami paper // planes
gliding and colliding.
It is of course, as we know, illusion,
construct of perception, memory and dreamings
and yet, its ravages pull inexplicably forward.
It is precious few and excessively many
years in a tumble,
days a dizzy,
long hours torturous or taken too fast,
and perfect, in their temporary majesty:
moments,
shined like a lover's smiling exhale,
naked and free on soft earth and singing breeze.
It is a particular gift waiting to be recognized as such.
Ever present,
patience endless.

My eyes are the same as my hands:
oceans,
waiting for their shorelines.

My body, it is a bent flower,
is a wide lake at sunrise,
is a mountain
         of strength
         of shake and tremble.

It is the silhouette of dancers,
is wild creature,
is beast wandered too far into desert.
It is spring grass and snow freeze,
is chained laughs and birds free,
is the endless stretch of river towards
the promise of an open sea.
It is tired.
It is trying.
It is a bowl continually polished
held aloft in beggars hands.

My spirit. My soul?
It is an ember, a coal.
Often flicker, sometimes flame.
Diamond of love,
hope without question,
wonder and wishes of wellness for the world.
It is a child's handprint of paint slapped on paper
and held up with awe to glow against all that sky.

For Once

Find a way to love your body

with all of its glorious imperfections.
With each ill-perception you have understandably,
but mistakenly
believed to be a truth.

Know that *your* body is a marvel
of divine and worthy architecture.

Set aside every ache and tremble,
just for a small moment,
each point of consternation,
every place you want to somehow heal or fix or shape
and just love the whole damn lot of you
exactly how it is.

Deeper and Deeper

Commit to love.
Again.
And again.
And always.

Let this white-hot radiance take all the sky.
There is no room for doubt in a universe
brimming with such effulgent beauty,
just look at those stars.

Every pore across the canvass of your skin a mirror,
a perforation of and for divinity, drinking in
love,
when you laugh,
flower petals drop like a sparkler's brigade of light
from the warmth under your tongue.
When you're weeping,
parched lands raise their hands in wonder
for the blessings of a rain.
When an anger rises,
the spirit of Warrior calls out for change;
be judicious in your actions but not afraid
to learn to burn.

Can you understand,
there is no particle of your holy being,
no emotion grand or small,
not a single, fleeting minute of your life
which is not worthy and welcome in this world.

The deeper you smile, the more you shine,
a sweet gift every time

like a kiss planted to the forehead.
The deeper you allow your sorrow,
how okay it is;
how brave and fierce to feel and to heal in letting go
and these holes carved out of you,
each one a sacred chamber meant for music.
Be patient,
from the darkness there is magic which will take you.

My love,
when you live
as open as you can to all which flows to and through you,
this heart
it cannot help
but beat to wonder.

Smoke and Mirrors

      Let me not forget to continue to hold space
for Spirit.
Let my own soft heart continue to be kneaded.
Let this body,
born witness to so much sorrow,
start to remember more
of the wildflowers it has also come to know.
      I have sweated,
running scared up to a mountain top
all in darkness
forgetting in my fright that eyes adjust,
that one can still see if you take the time to look,
that shadows hold so much beauty
a menagerie of stories,
forgetting that the devil's best trick was to convince us
Fear
has any sort of power greater than our hearts.
      Hold my hand,
take a breath with me,
we will step into these fires together.
Ten thousand of your fathers, mothers,
sisters and brothers
have walked through these wilds
uncountable times before.
The fact that you are alive right now
is proof undivided that your blood still screams
and sings to discover.
There are warriors, poets, dreamers, teachers,
builders, dancers, and lovers each standing inside of you;
having gone through ages of challenge
and passed down all their wisdom,

it roars now a fierce and tender dragon
in every molecule of your DNA.
And the darkness
it is not so troubling after all;
it is an old hat trick,
sleight of hand,
puff of smoke behind which
        Fear is revealed
to be a friend—
sitting patiently,
begging to help you grow.
Why else would he stay with you for so long?
Meet his eyes and smile,
step up,
the secrets he points the way towards
are all worth more than gold.
He opens doors to your soul so you may share it even brighter.
Every time you rise to greet him with a tender smile,
with a brave willingness,
do not worry,
you will grow lighter.

Reframe

If you require a reason for joy
you may be waiting a very long time.
Or,
you could choose one for yourself,
right now.

Are not the emerald crowns of trees
swaying like dancers against the stage of the sky
reason enough to smile?

The decision is your own,
every moment ripe
and open for reinterpretation.

Dawn Song

A crow hops on one midnight foot,
warble of birds faint around
every point of the compass.
Breeze stirs cool against me,
cross-legged on this lone bench
built for gathering perspective.
The sky of course proves it mastery
as always, unconcerned with anything but creation.
This time shows a band of stark rose
lying low to the left,
eases through a few peach electric streaks
before it softens and spreads into dusty-
blue-yellow-lavender on the outer edges of horizon.

Dawn sings.
Every time.

Your heart holds its own senses,
listen with more than just your mind.
All this magic
blossoms
in just a few precious moments,
unique, stunning
and always
so available.
The bay waters drink it in,
what a life—
to dress in such new finery every day!
We see only
the luminous, embroidered reflection
but imagine, for a moment,

how deeply beneath the colors seep.
Every inch of 3D space
a crimson prism to swim through,
a world softly imbued with scintillating hue.
      So your heart
it is shined
in much the same fashion,
every cloud you might hold
lit up and gold,
every cold corner suddenly swept
with light.
      The dawn sings.
The sky opens.
Miles of the faintest pearl-pink
stretch out before you,
behind,
above
and inside.
      Be still here.
Breathe and believe
in the magic that is offered.
Let yourself savor,
let your heart
also rise.

Lantern

There is a part of me which
will never stop singing.
Hope holds tired a captive heart
and for the most part
I say thank you for this,
long as the nights may stretch sometimes.
It is a gift to remember the stars I have learned to follow,
to close my eyes in gratitude
even as a weary soul grows more so in a weary world.
But I came here with a diamond coal
indestructible in the core
of my being;
a song of such furious hope
and knowledge of the love that weaves
the world together,
and I say thank you for this,
from my dark and lonely corners,
for the part of me
which can never stop singing.

Pandemic

And a falcon leaps
suddenly
down from these gold-dusted sunset branches.

What loft he finds,
wind screaming strongly,
yet it only helps him rise.
I watch
as wings spread wide he is lifted, gliding
so far through a moment
infused only
with light.

And a small part of my heart
it is carried.

I find a little less lonely.

I don't know so much what to say nowadays,
this year just a haze,
every morning the world in such tremble
and My God I miss dancing,

to take all this weight
and move it away with abandon,
finding lift
releasing spirit
paving the path for joy
as music becomes moment stretched shining into presence
and breathless connection.

And my god I miss loving,
sometimes so hard it feels like I'm dying

and I'm trying,
to keep this heart flying in a hundred small moments,
I am sorry
if so often I forget to say it,
know that I do.

And Twin Peaks' shadow now stretches
more than halfway across this city,
the sun is reclining,
the falcon given way to ravens'
black wings glinting in the distance.

Soon the windows on the hillside
will catch the last of the hour,
becoming God's welcoming campfires
shined golden amber
for just a moment more.

Around the Corner

Perhaps the very reasons you feel so unworthy of love
are exactly why you deserve
and require it most of all.
Perhaps those fears which keep you trapped
and all the rest that holds you back
was never your fault.
Perhaps you just need a little more
of some sweet force
and you were never broken,
just in loss.
Maybe it's okay that you're still lost.
Maybe the stars and the cards
and the rolls of the dice in the darkest of nights
still hold a surprise of light from God's dreams
to awaken some shining scene you've never seen before.
Maybe better and best still are yet to come.
Maybe your path is so damn different for good reasons.
Maybe sooner than later you'll figure out exactly what you need to.
Maybe you'll make friends with every ghost.
Maybe the songs that will be sung to you
will speak of truths you've known
but never had a glimmer how to show,
maybe all those sweet reflections you have needed still
are on their way.

This Sacred Fire

I'll hold it for you, always.
Come when you are tired.
Come when you are cold.
Come when the weight
of the world
or even simply your own precious life
falls unnecessarily heavy upon your shoulders.
Touch my hands,
I'll open my eyes like sunrise,
kiss your forehead,
there is no other home than here.

Take a breath and let me warm you,
sit by my side and we will marvel
at a glittering sky.
When you are weary,
when your bones shake,
when your time feels like a cage
around your heart
let me remind you;
with a hug,
with a smile,
with a brush of my fingertips against your temple,
that you are loved—
deeply,
and forever.

Take a breath and let me hold you.
There is room here for any ocean you may be.
For every quake and tremor,
for any shadows you are still afraid to see.

There is room here,
I promise,
a soft and secret hearth slip next to,
Love,
just breathe.

There is, nestled between mountain and sky, a meadow
peppered with wild birds and luminous flowers,
each one waiting to sing
and to shine
towards whichever shattered pieces you have need to rest.

Sit by my fire,
we'll share songs.
Whisper if you have to,
I will carry your heart until it feels again
strong enough to rise.

Patience

Brave through the winter,
stay for the gold.

—The breaking of a heart
                open

NO

       Today I will not fall prey
to more spiraling dissonance
with my words.
Today
I will fake it,
because despite a whirlwind
of contrary experience I still
may choose
to trust
in love.
       Because a thousand friends' lips all
drop rose petals when they speak
behind my back,
because I am cared for even when I am
care-less,
because the decision is mine to make.
I have been hurt,
sometimes I am forced to live there,
and still this being human comes with
so much shattering beauty
if only we will choose to see.
       Watch out my window
as a homeless man tucks in another
with his own threadbare jacket,
a gold-leafed flower defies its lack of earth and springs
from a concrete wasteland,
my own mother besieged with troubles
laughs and talks of love every time
we have ever spoken.
Every.
Time.

I am blessed beyond measure,
and today I will exercise my god-power of focus to remember.
Despite depression,
despite pain,
despite echoes and worries,
frustrations and failures,
despite dragons that still gnaw every dawn
on this battered blood pump,
today I will fake it.
I will look towards what shimmers.
Today I allow myself to trust
that more is possible than we might ever know or feel.
Today I will choose
to say
Thank You
for all moments which have shown my spirit
just how much of a brilliant ocean
it can be.

The Safety of Familiar Stings

How addicted we human love creatures are
to melancholy
to the sadness
to the loneliness,
to the idea that to become better and bright
we must be built of pieces only others offer.
          I too
so often am guilty of such a crime against myself,
of selling this soul off simply because
it appears too much to bear.
But I am trying to remember differently,
to remind this weary familiarity
that the bigger I allow myself to be instead,
the more gravity will serve me.
The more light will bend and curve in my direction,
the more magic I will attract
simply by standing shoreline strong.
          To smile in gratitude even on the days that crumble,
because crying is easy
missing is easy
wishing is so easy it becomes a habit,
becomes a pattern,
becomes a life lived as a testament
only to what isn't there,
instead of a reality created
by recognition of everything we have
been gifted.
          The truth is we are afraid
to feel differently,
our pains so close, familiar and comfortable.
We cling to them like wreckage

from a ship still keeping us afloat.
But still keeping us held down.
We are more afraid of the unknown
and so
we return time and again to our own hollow
instead of being willing to let go.
       Let go.
Grow.
Swim wild as far into that blinding sunrise as you can.
Kiss your aches softly
but do not sacrifice yourself
for the safety of their ancient harbor
Be thankful.
Be brave.
The world is begging for you.

MY Guest House

To Hopelessness,
Pointlessness,
Lethargy,
Fear,
Collapse,
Sadness,
Longing,
Desperation,
to all these important parts of the human experience:

YOU HAVE OUTGROWN YOURSELF.
You have outgrown yourself.
You have outgrown yourself
and you WILL
return to more balanced proportions.

This is a guest house yes,
but you have overstayed your welcome.

Do I not maintain the grounds,
sweep the floors,
clean the rooms?
Do I not keep a fire burning,
listen to your stories,
wake every single morning to greet you?

You have outlasted your invitation.
You have been living
in a place meant to hold so many
but you,
for too long a time,
have left nowhere near enough room
for all other vibrant wanderers to visit.

I am kicking you out.
I am reclaiming space.

Am I not the master of this house?
Am I not the Master of this house!

You are no longer permitted to remain here,
not when your mess extends to every corner.
This is a way station for you and all your kin,
but not a residence,
but not your home.

Consider this an eviction notice.

Pack up your sorrows,
pull your weight from the shelves,
take your shadows and your oceans,
patch the holes
in MY walls
that you've left,
and repaint them.
You were not meant to live here.

You stay up too late,
you get up too early,
you never stop talking.
You have taken advantage
and convinced me that I am here to serve you.

Wake The Fuck Up,
get the FUCK out,
this is my house
and I am here to welcome you but not
to provide for you.

Instead of teaching,
you have filled these halls with drama,
and I will no longer entertain
this profligate consumption of my resources,

get the fuck out.

There are too many spirits waiting
to come in from the cold:

Joys and Angers.
Curiosity and Wonder and Awe.
Disgust and Pride
and Strength and Delight
and Fury and Fierceness and Ease
and Presence,
and Trust and Power and Courage.
Determination and Faith and Wisdom,
Frustration and Cheer
and Hope.
          And Pleasure.
                    And Love.

There is a full spectrum in stagnation,
an entire pantheon
aching to share the treasures
they cultivate from the world,

and you have been holding me hostage
inside the very rooms I work so hard
for all of us to live in.

Get. Out.

To Depression.
To Loneliness.

To Longing.
To Fear that no longer protects,

this is my life,
this is my future,
this is My Fucking House.

And you are always welcome to visit,
but you are no longer allowed to stay.

Tributary

There is an ocean
to which all rivers run
and not a single one
is ever refused.

Can you understand this?

You could turn your head away
the entirety of life,
walk caustic, stubborn, blind
and still.
   And still.
     And still
always,

always be welcomed home.

Anandamaya

Kiss these aches softly and let them go.
A boat made out of an acorn and a feather
set adrift under moonlight
with a whisper, a wish and a prayer
given back to a world that has room
to hold all the shame we no longer need to on our own.

And the deepest parts of you that feel shame
are the most beautiful,
Darling.

These broken, gentle giants.
These young rivers muddled.
These lost boys weeping.
These rough-hewed creatures.
These wrongs felt unforgivable.
These titanic fists turned inwards against
what we have understandably, but incorrectly believed
mistaken about our very natures.
All these wretched scars, sorrows, needs
and brutally perceived bits and pieces;

These we will build monuments of light to,
weave crowns of flowers every day
and lay them with mother-love across our most hidden
hope- and helpless faces.
This destitution we will hold in our arms
long after the night has fallen,
singing songs and tender lullabies,
gazing into eyes bereft
with the blazing warmth of ten thousand summer suns.

Each moment that we believe unmade us,
we will carry
as a holy treasure

from the dark caves of a mind taught not to know any better
to the open sea of our hearts which are
the deepest manifestation of every song God wakes to.
          There is no man or woman
mother or father
beating, rape, death, addiction or destruction
that can take away
the glory of morning blossom that you were born to be.
Underneath all suffocating shadows,
however deep and long the suffering,
is your sweet-child-heart and wonder
wounded yes,
but still immutably golden,
simply aching for love
and you

are Divinely Worthy.
Full stop.
You are Divinely Worthy.
Deep breath.
You are Divinely Worthy.

          Take a hand to your own breast
regardless of strength or tremble
and rest it there,
feel its soft weight
and your rising breath
and trust
that the dust which has choked too many of your moments
is just that,
just dust.

One tired layer,
a ragged, heavy coat,
wet feathers, shedding skin,
old stories
to be shaken off so the rest of you can shine.
You are Golden.
You are Golden.
You are Golden.
        You are love, beaten back perhaps but
never diluted,
traumatized, taught and programmed to believe
you are less but
—belief—
is a creature,
can be tamed like any other.
Befriended, shown new ways to live,
come in now,
come in from the cold.
        Treat yourself as a wounded traveler,
as a puppy from the pound;
given care, a heart and a home
how they heal, every time.
You can do this.
You are golden.
You were wounded and
you are still golden.
You are divinely worthy, my love,
you are deserving
as every poor creature hurting,
of deep rest and the time to heal.

My love,
you precious, tender and beautiful child
you are golden.

You will heal.

You will not live inside these pains forever.

You are the glitter of stars timeless
in a smooth and shining sea.

So Much Room

Come into this heart.

The door swings open gently

        when you sing.

     When you quiet.

When you breathe

there is
always
another chance.

And another.
And another.

Take your time.

Gather your pieces:

Those tears of the child who could not understand
and his laughter unabashed
which you long to remember.

Take those jagged edges of your broken hearts
and hold them softly,
though you tremble,
know the warmth of your life now
and the swell of this earth beneath your feet
is all the strength you need.

Take your prayers, wishes, dreams,
all that you have seen,
take what starts you dancing.

Take your music,
that unique and precious intonation of your voice
into the wind,
remember there are more hearts than you will ever know
that soften when they hear you.

Take your anger,
your pride,
your sorrow,
take the fury and the failure
take betrayals,
all in the cupped palm of your naked and wild soul,

There is So Much Room
Beloveds,
to set every shaking worry on the altar
with the grace of love.

Take your shivers, your pleasures,
your whispers to the singing stars
and these too rest before you,
into this heart.
This shining, crying and beautiful knowing heart of yours.
In one hand it beats the drum
of your individual and perfect expressive nature,
and in the other it pumps the blood
of all things this universe aches to know,
hold back nothing.

These hands are yours and at the same time, God's.
Can you understand the expanse of horizon
which unfolds its petals continuously within you?

Come deeper.
Don't be frightened.
Be held,
love,
there is no ground to crash into,
just this wild and welcoming space
like a bloom of sunrise
or the diamond curtain of starshine strewn across silk.

You can fly, you can fall, you can soar,

take your time.

Take another breath.

Come back
to this heart

Love,

take as many chances as you need.

The Silence Between Heartbeats

I will write for you ten thousand poems.
A small snowstorm,
a flurry of gold leaves dropping,
the claps from a standing ovation.
A field of poppies,
a field of puppies,
all in hopes that even just one beautiful word
will find the gap betwixt your thoughts and interpretation
to butterfly kiss your soul.

BrainHeartBoneCage

You are starshine.
Dear Human.
Dear Human Form.
You are a great white light beast all
butterfly lightning wings and angel claws,
all glow and shimmer packed down with brilliance into
this brain heart bone cage but
remember
your expanse.
You wild,
you thunder,
you gold-petaled flower forever kaleidoscope opening in void.
Dear Human.
Dear Human Illusion.
You are no more these sorrows
than you were those triumphs the time before.
You are no more these struggles
than you are the daydream which preceded them no,
you are more.
Above, below and beyond this mind skin blood frame you
are the big-bang raging;
a whirl of rainbows,
a tumult of tireless, observing love,
a pair of grand, luminous wings stretching beyond the sky condensed
into this body for a time you are
consciousness in motion.
You are a universe dancing,
dear Human.
Dear Human Creature.
You beam,
you light strength pillar,

you divine shock troop have come to ravel so much forgotten
you find yourself full of holes only
to let more of your own radiance pour out of you, remember:
there is nothing but new truths to be gained,
experience is a game we have chosen to play,
gratitude is the air we breathe,
love is waiting in every moment to feed you.
       Dear human,
dear Human God:
remember, you are nothing less.

To Fill This Space

So much more beauty to come.

I don't even have room for it all right now.

Golden hooves,
arctic snow
and red-velvet blankets to lay on in it.

Warmth to make me feel worthy of being a prince.

One perfect dew drop on the tip of a leaf.

Ten thousand sunrises and all their pretty music,

SO MUCH MORE BEAUTY TO COME.

Glorious, fabulous, fantastic delights,
petals unfurling
light pink and the kiss
of a butterfly landing.

A fireplace and a rug before it,
and guitar in the background
and ease,
a feeling like floating
knowing everything is ok.

So much more beauty to come
to fill
this empty space
I will not fail
to hold my chambers open,

my blood warm, rushing and pushing the air—
simply sun transformed—
to every inch and sense of mine.

I will be strong
until the times comes when I may be soft again,

so much more beauty to come.

Anxiety

There is so much, and I'd rather be
in hammocks swinging endlessly,
ten thousand dreams of wanderings,
a songbird's dawn-ripe melodies.

I'd rather feel your hands on me,
our bodies blending energies,
those eyes alight with love shining,
we: drifting wish on gentle breeze.

And turquoise skies clouds dallying,
sun sprawled on sea so sparkly,
the air out there I'd beg to breathe
more pure and clear than anything.

I'd rather see you smiling
and melt into your whisperings,
those eyes so wide with possiblies,
our fingertips' soft tremblings.

Root down in forest's mysteries,
refresh beneath the canopy,
the stillness held within the trees,
this soothing, dappled reverie.

I'd rather take this heart beating,
roll gentle as a leaf downstream,
an eagle soaring effortlessly,
warm glow of fire, flickering.

If you could reach this heart beating,
put breath to neck and softly sing,
I might forget these troublings,
remember how to let life be.

If you could reach this heart beating,
wrap arms around, lean into me,
this chest may still its quivering,
this mind may rest and start to dream

and there will be some days when I won't spin.

The Truth

All my words are prayers
all my prayers are heard
all my songs are love
all my life is song.

Swingin' Around

I'll pick you up and swing you around
we'll never come down
never come down,
      we won't touch the ground
          we won't touch the ground
             we won't
                  touch the ground.

Little kid legs flying through the air
and a smile on your face wide
as a birthday grin

and this ocean we are,
under blooming rose of morning sun

becoming steam,
becoming light becoming
big fluffy daydream storybook clouds drifting,
becoming something new
and golden.
Becoming simple magic to behold.
Becoming a treasure to be kept in front pockets
and marveled at out in the schoolyard at recess.
Becoming marbles,
three of 'em,
and the little rainbows they cast on little fingers
when held into the light.
Becoming a found red feather,
a rusty key dug from the earth and all
its possibilities
becoming sacred,
becoming known and wonder,

a nest in a nook of a tree
and the cracked little fragments of eggshells blue
as your sweet child eyes.
Becoming young again
in your heart,
free as those summer vacation somedays
when the long hours left you all sticky and dirty and rich,
when you and the world were no separate bodies,
just a tumbling climbing running lounging exploring
expression of each other's joy.

And worry, my love,
this is an invitation to let worry drift out the window.

What was can be held again,
you are still a creature.
You are so much more than thought and trying
you are still
Creature.
Still bone, blood and muscle,
scent and soil,
still dusk and leaves and loam
and mountain.
And jungle.
And desert.
Still roar and song and paw and wag and claw
and cave
and lightning, still
light
and warmth and heart and heat,
still raw
wild
untamed creative love waiting to explore,

let yourself.

Let yourself be.

Take your bare feet to the grass,
to the sand by the sea,
dip your toes in
feel the breeze
and breathe.
Believe me when I tell you that freedom
is just a wish away.
A song,
a dance,
a giggle,
a sitting down
and a setting down,
for a just a moment,
all the weight that you have carried.
All the fear that you have been tricked into thinking
was ever more real than the feel
of the day on your face,
or the stars winking while you wait
to see that streak of one falling
and blazing your wish across the sky.

Climb into these arms again.
The world is waiting to hold you
and give you all the gifts you've ever thought were lost.
There is nothing more to figure out,
my love,
you are home now.

You always were.

And we'll swing around,
around and around,
our feet off the ground

we'll never come down.
    we'll never come down.
        We'll never
            not ever,
                not ever come down.

Listen, Please

Can I tell you a secret?

Every warm joy lives
forever inside of you.
Close your eyes and remember.

Can I tell you another?

Every last tremble and heartache
can be given
with love
to the world outside your body.

There is so much room.

Let go.

The sky and the ocean,
heaven and earth,
wait to embrace all pains you
are willing to release.

Let go.

Can I tell you one last?

You are loved,

deeply and forever.

After the Breaking

Your holes are your own,
Honey,
any mortar another may mash together will only
crumble when you are alone
you know,
we can only fix ourselves.

And baby you're supported!
By a thousand hands, hearts and smiles
all shining huge in your direction,
but even the ground can not tell you how to walk
or run or jump
Honey,
we'll always be here when you stumble
but you'll have to change
yourself.

Take those tears and sweat a little,
find your blood and make it rush.

What do you love?
Start here.
What did you love?
Start there.

The couch, the bed, the distance into which you stare
is open-ended,
a hole which has no depth,
stagnation—
don't stay long.

You've made it this far,
you are strong.

By will, and patience, carry on,
every darkness has a dawn,
Dear,
keep on dreaming.
Remember you are loved
Dear,
cherished like no other by a chain of souls
all here to hold you.
Remember how much joy you've felt
through other times,
remember all the smiles you've been given,
and the light which you have sparked
in so many people's lives.

Remember you are whole even with these fractures
Honey,
more beautiful by far from every ache and scar
that's so far shaped you,
which even now are teaching you your strength.

Such heavy lifting seems impossible,
I know,
I've done a fair share of my own
been bent to breaking,
found myself in tears and shaking
more times than I can count.
But every space which has been hollowed out
has only carved more room
for me to hold more light.
Honey,
you can do this.

Even such a pain of emptiness can still be held
with love.

Treat yourself tender.
Nourish all the broken things
you have been wanting from another.
We can see your holes and share our stories
but only your own soul
can brave the depths and raise the magic
'til you're whole again.

What are you grateful for?
Start here.
What were you grateful for?
Start there.

Pick a tiny point of light
and find your focus.
Honey,
you can do this.
Trust this,
know this.
You will return to bright.

Song to Fill the Silence

My heart for you.

My sticky secrets,
spilled wine,
scarred over scratches in the thick
crimson walls of its hollow and hallowed caverns.
This brimming essence
and unshakeable endless rivers by which it rushes,
flowing of, to, from, through and for love,
always.
This ceaseless pattern of drum and pulsation
that clocks all moments and surrenders.
Each chamber and its hidden wonders
laid bare for you.
Take a journey, and a trinket when you go,
there is so much treasure to be held here,
gardens and their overpowering fruit dropping
bombs of intoxicating sweetness.
Take a bite, eat your fill.

There is room here and more.
Find the shade from trees which still grow strong,
even after all those storms.
Take me with you as you rest a cheek
and that soft crop of curls upon my chest.

There is drifting,

Remind me of the space that I have cultivated,
and the peace in the pause to the pulse
that remains present beyond all
temporary experiences of participation in a life.

Take me with you into me,
for love is the wind.
And the heart is the sail.
And the body a battered boat painted brightly still
and this world an endless ocean to explore.
Take me with you into me,
for love is the question,
the answer,
and the song which fills the silence in between.
And the heart,
it is the organ upon which all music plays
and plays

and plays.

Cabin

I have come
for my place in the sun.
To unwind
molecule by molecule
allowing space to blossom,
to let my breath take the shape
of the world into my bones,
to sit here,
right here,
nested in the grass,
to feel at home.

This body is my treasure:
my temple,
my grail,
my great ship
sailing through a life.
What shores have I yet to visit?
What strange sights and secret beauties,
what storms will I get to witness,
climbing high into the crows nest and
screaming my own heart wild
to become one with the sea
in all repose or furor?

I can change one thing
and one thing only:
My Self,
my timber.
Let every step then be taken
with gratitude.

May every breath be recognized
as a gift I am blessed to partake of.
May I choose to honor myself and all
that I have danced with
in every moment
may I grow deeper
in love
with the beauty that surrounds us.
May I fortify my vessel,
may I be courageous in strange winds.
May I turn towards the sun's sets and rises,
breathing deep into vibrance which is freely offered
every day
may I learn to be guided by the strong currents
flowing around me.
In every moment
may I treasure kindness,
may I dwell with bravery
may I find ease, and stillness.

May I sit in the cabin of the heart,
moving through this world,
eyes wide with wonder.

Transformation

Light does not simply chase away darkness,

It absorbs it. Dissolves it.
Takes darkness in its loving hands and sings
sweetly until sublimation;

and then shadows themselves become
new expressions of grace.

(Your love is light.)

Sunrise on Tank Hill

Clumps of small grass,
strands pointed tall and
the red-brown earth between their fingers.
In this dawn light as each blade
glows like a rising saint,
it is another moment gifted
to remember
the sacred in the ordinary.

If Gods are anywhere
then they are everywhere,
whispering:

Look here!
      Look here,
            look here...

Look how your shadow stretches a half mile
from this hilltop over quiet patchwork rooftops,
did you forget
the grandiosity of your being
and all its capacity to reach for?

Look at these chestnut birds
each no bigger than a golf ball,
how they flit and flicker
amongst a garden of rocks all manner of shapes
no mathematician could ever name.
How they never stop searching
and never stop singing.

Look at this bench,
holding the entirety of you.
The five thick lines of its long lean boards,
the inch of space between each,
the geography of hillside glimpsed beneath,
a scatter of flowers no bigger than thumbnails
opened joyfully,
their size irrelevant to their depth of dedication
to the ripe new day.

Look at this world.
Look at all it has made for you,
all that it waits for you to notice,
all that it prays with to remind you
how to love.

Look at your life,
if you can,
when you can,
with the same quiet marvel.

The geography of your hands,
all they have held and passed over.

The songs your heart has sung
as it shakes, shivers, surrenders
and celebrates over the years.

That beautiful face of yours,
how your loved ones glow
to see it smile.

Muni

The boy in the red jacket with a green balloon
and his dad with a hula-hoop and the way they lean
into each other in the bus seats
like a rowboat with its dock on the lakeshore.

And there are rainbows on the floor from the sun
through this window through an old woman's glasses,
she smells like mall perfume you can tell she feels
       so lovely
and I love her.

And there are three languages coming from the back:
Japanese,
Spanish,
another I cannot place.

There are such beautiful tides of life
taking this ride to all manner of destinations,
there are thirty-five pairs of shoes
and thirty-five souls in motion.

When it is sunny out people talk to each other more,
recognizing warmth.

I want the light to be bright in my eyes always,
so I can see everybody's halos more clearly,
so I will not be afraid
to talk to strangers.

Interdependence

We smile at each other.
It's not that hard but it is scary at first,
having learned so early on to never
talk to strangers.
Her face is drawn up tightly
so I offer up a grin
as kindly as I can to let her know she's seen,
and it's contagious,
the softening,
how she decompresses in her seat
and starts to breathe
more deeply.
I can see,
she is not so used to kindness,
not as much as she deserves.
I smile wider
from seats away,
place a hand on my heart and tilt my head
in reverence,
and those eyes of hers they fill
with fresh spring blooms.

The Gathering

On the first day
we danced
until there was nothing else but sacred movement.
Our feet were the ground
and the earth became our bodies
and into the night the fire
snap roared leapt
and our shadows left
to become wild things,
joining hands we were dark and flesh and sweat
and holy.

On the second day
we wept.
Some of us became oceans
some rivers,
my own body ballooned and shrank—
an iceberg softening,
remembering its ancient form.
We lost
all that we needed to:
ghosts and demons,
sorrows and secrets
and old, old defenses ready to be finally retired.
In a circle of arms on shoulders
we watered the cool soil,
we were brave and humbled and bare,
we were naked and unashamed and together,
seeing the same pains written across all our faces
we gave our hearts to the center,
and were holy.

On the third day
we laughed,
held in our hands golden bells,
a thousand swinging wildly.
We threw back our heads,
let our mouths parade open,
crawled out of our own skin and transformed;
there were lions there
and wolves
and giant birds
and tumbling children
and colors shimmering like sunlight across a clear lake.
We felt our bellies rumble and rolled wild
across the land
it was a celebration,
we shook with satisfaction,
hooted and hollered and
hop skipped knee slapped cracked up and panting,
growing smiles like fireworks,
delighted
and holy.

And on the last day,
we sat,
silent and sturdy as the thousand year Sequoia.
Our breaths constant as the tide,
eyes closed we opened our
minds clear we listened our
hearts wide we loved,
and the song of the spirits
in silence
rose up through us.

We rested, poised and peaceful
and the softest sigh escaped our lips collectively,
a breeze across the meadow as the sun stretches his first fingers
long through the dew.
We were mountains rooted,
strong and full of wonder,
ready to cradle all the sky,
we became light
beams drifting through an emerald canopy.
We were stone,
hands clasped,
sweet guardian sentries immutable
in contemplation and serenity
we were human,
creatures fresh, silent and new as the dawn
which washed over us.
We were present,
together,
extensions of the deepest hearts of love,
we were holy.

10,000 Types of Music

On this morning
the traffic is perfectly oceanic
out my window.
The ebb and rise,
the swell and fading roar-rush-purr
of blurred rubber spun against slick asphalt
makes a lull that pulls me

                                     miles

                            miles

                            out to sea.

Close my eyes and the occasional bus
roaring to life after catching its breath
at a stoplight
is the crest of one surprisingly towering wave
crashing back into the symphony.

I want so much to make every moment mean something.

This brain tries hard to alchemize,
to wrest gold from simple fruit
instead of practicing the truth
of just letting the world be
what it is,

ten thousand types of music.

This Topography of Life

You deserve to smile for no reason
other than the world delights you.

A flash of flower color radiant in sun spray,
snippet of song slips up from school days
sing it,
sing it loud and be merry.
This life is not just for lessons and the inevitable hardship,
cliches of the broken artist,
so much more it is meant for—
Joy!
For you to revel and experience
the uncountable blessings of the senses
and how each one can make your heart dance inside your chest.

The sparkle of dawn through window corner,
tea-steam whispering of comfort,
sink your teeth through the soft sunrise flesh of a fresh nectarine
and feel
the burst of juices spilling over.
Run your hand along the wall like a child as you walk,
each fingertip receiving.
What is texture?

This topography of life
it is so safe to get lost in
remember,
what it's like to whirl and giggle,
dash under the crystalline arc of a garden hose in summer—
thick, cold drops splashed on your back
till the grass catches your laughter.
A true smile springs through surrender,
you can choose to do so much more often than we're taught to.

Raise your face to the sun in welcome,
your atoms spin faster,
every space between them widens to rejoice in light.

This is a prayer.

A holy sacrament of life,
this is the promise.
There is always warmth to find
turn towards it.

And rains come, of course.
Storms will be heard
and hard,
you will have many scars,
each of these too can be a treasure.
In your boundless unfolding heart,
canyons carved
and deserts dusty
all are just another part of the landscape
that your life becomes.
These will never define you.
There are forests, oceans, mountains, and gardens too.
Pick a flower, wander to the edge of the abyss
make a wish
and let it go.

The sound of silence does not have to drown
but crowns a stillness,
opens to a quiet breath,
there's beauty to be found in every facet,
bow your head
and welcome.

To Grow Full

I read
        a lovely poem,
                small and
                        short.
It glittered,
        how the sun taps his fingertips
        upon the quiet ocean.

Most poems, if you get right down to it
        simply ask you to pay attention.

        Or better,
                        they invite you.

How the coffee fills and foams,
        chestnut ochre.

How this sweet grandmother,
        small and
                short,

        sets herself down
                contentedly
                        on a faded green bench.
        Her feet hang like a child's in the air,
                she swings them slowly.

What is it you see in this life?
        What do you smell, taste, touch, hear,

                                        feel?

On any given day

(on *every*)

to grow full requires so much less
than we are taught.

Pick your delights ripe from
the cornucopia of moments.

Take as much as you are wanting.

Take all that you may need.

All That has Been Given

The bulb and the light,
the grass and the sky,
a spoon and the smooth, cool weight
      of the handle which enters my grasp.
These two palms,
      the creases within them,
      the rivers beneath them of blood
      rushing.
A heart, pumping,
      all that it feels, has felt,
      this yearning ever for love
      in as many ways as it is possible
      to know.
Mothers.
      Fathers.
          Siblings.
             Lovers.
               Friends.
Wheels on the car
      and the radio to sing to
      as we road trip towards adventure.
The mix of stone that makes the road,
      the tall tall tall tall tree
      that we pause next to.
The music of a bird dropping down
      to meet us.
The hand on our shoulder
      from a grandmother,
      her smile to remember.

The reminder of preciousness,
       through impermanence
       by passage through the door
       nobody returns from.
The thin tickle of wet salt
       rolling from an eye.
Color,
       this parade of color every moment
       of a life.
A cozy blanket,
       a well-loved book,
          a glass of cool water.
The turning of Earth
       to wake up the day
over
       and over
          and over.

Every Breath

Every one of my words is a prayer.
Every step.
Every breath inside this sacred cave
          beneath my breast.
Every tear I have loosed,
          dried salt blown to a billowy sky,
every whisper released
          in a trembling night.
Every scream is a prayer,
every howl,
every cry,
every song I have danced to
          is spirit in flight.
Every sigh that I've taken,
every hug I have shared,
every hand I have shaken,
every fear I have bared.
Every moment I move through
is an offering to love,
is gratitude gifted,
is a humble bow at the opportunity to be here,
          experiencing any part of this great mystery
          at all.
Each one of my words
is a prayer

          to be Seen
          to be Heard
          to be Felt

to be Given
to Give
to Love,
and to Live

in the majesty of a world
that is bigger, kinder and more beautiful
than ever we could know.

Hafiz: "We Have Not Come Here to Take Prisoners"

And this,
this is a poem my soul wants
        to hear every morning upon waking,
these are the words I want whispered
        to my dreams while I am sleeping,
this is a poem I want every one of my cells to take
        turns writing in each other's DNA.
These are words I want to teach all my children
        and their children
        and all their friends,
this is the kind of truth I want to draw close to
        when I bite into that sumptuous peach and grin,
        sticky with juice coursing down my chin
        and ruining another shirt
and I don't want to care
so much about anything
for

we have not come here to take prisoners.

And every failure and frustration,
        every lover and lost,
        every pain and
        every worry
we must release
        so there is room inside
        our questing hearts
        for much more joy to dance in.

And every joy and jubilation,
    every tiny miracle,
    every hug and hope
    and flash of wisdom
we must release,
        we must share so that each atom of this world
        is shined by the warm cloth of our smiles.

For we have not come here to take prisoners,

but to wonder like children grown dizzy on their backs
gaping as a flock of birds owns the sky.

And this is a poem worthy of being written in my skin by a needle.
These are words any Gods worthy of belief
        will set all their power helping us to remember.
This a poem to hold like a last letter from a lover against the heart,
this is a poem to be copied and cast off rooftops by the thousands
        into the wind for

we have not come here to take prisoners.

A Life of Prayer and Song

This book we are writing,
feathers and stone.
Rivers and thunder,
mountains and bone.

There is
a sacred blessing in every conscious breath.
There is
a doorway via gratitude,
a boundless field through giving thanks
in which the most tender of tinder
can be found
to keep a fire burning for the heart.
There is a resonance in movement,
cultivated flow,
dance like you are lightning born witness to land
for the first time.
Walk like you are a child
with a spring in your step,
with a curiosity
for what color every next moment will feed you.
There is grace in devotion
to a just cause.
There is redemption in forgiveness
no matter how deep the wound.
There is,
in compassion,
the true corridor to God.

How many times
have you been

the lone wolf howling—
for a pack,
for a path,
for a den,
for a meal?
Raise your voice in song
and show the world this love
you are aching to feel.

How many times
have you been—
the lost child,
crushed flower,
desperate sailor,
ship with no anchor,
creature roaming a bare desert?

There is
that Golden Rule:
Do Unto Others,
for truly,
they are you.
There are unexpected answers for all who seek,
there are uncollected colors for every secret dream,
there is magnificence
in holding reverence
every time you breathe.
There is power in simplicity,
in taking pause,
in presence,
in recognition of the world,

in acceptance of her lessons.
There is a bird with golden feathers winging high over your troubles.
There is a Friend who rises across the whole sky
to bring light
to your life
every day

there is always
another opportunity
to say I Love You,

to let the past become at last just a leaf melting on the path,
to look forward,
to lift your head and breathe, and smile.
To open the palms of your hands,
to greet the new day
as an old friend,
to welcome
all that is waiting to meet you.

There is a treasure of song in your heart,
your spirit is a ceaseless prayer,
and the sacred offering of life
is all this time you are given
to listen

and sing along.

Last Call

And should this be the end

I will soar
eagle high,
give my last calls
like a shaman
to the wind,
dance all mud-heavy
and rain dressed.
I will run
like a wild thing
and boogie,
and should this be the end

I will fire my volleys
of laughter
into the abyss.
I will tear off
my clothes
and splash
into the ocean.
I will be a creature
and I will be free
to be taken
back to the tide
and should this be the end

I will spin dreamwebs
and reel you in
with my stories.
Flame bright
my eyes
will warm you,

fallen foes
and friends alike,
let my ink-stained palms
paint you pictures
of another glowing night.
Let my fingertips
trace comet trails
and draw roadmaps in the sky
from stars
to lands of freedom
and should this be the end

I will clear a circle,
roll up stones for our seats
and invite you in.
Sit by me
by the fire
and share my blanket,
it was hand woven by grandmothers
whose every wrinkle
is a chuckle
from a soul such as ours.
Let our observations of the night
be like the night:
warm and mellow.
Let the slow cadence of the drums
soften us
and prepare the way
and should this be the end

let us lean in
to each other,
and watch love reflected
through flames dancing
one last time,
together.

Acknowledgments

To thank every beloved in my life who has inspired these poems would fill a book all of its own. But I have to offer a deepest bow of gratitude to those specifically who've made it possible for *A Life of Prayer & Song* to finally enter the world:

Brianna Schnaubelt, my staggeringly talented sister whose watercolor paintings grace the covers... Have I told you lately??

Finn Deerheart, my champion supporter whose words of eloquent distillation fill the back cover.

Jeanette Encinias, fellow heart-poet, who kickstarted this entire project with her wisdom and discernment.

Susi Clark of Creative Blueprint Design, who gave the book its true form and guided me with such care through self-publication.

Ocean Finlay, for being a MotherFuckin Sparkle Beast aiding all my odds and ends.

Myself, for caring, believing, creating, and loving.

My teachers, my teacher's teachers, and all their teachers, through millennia of discovering and sharing ways to Be.

To connect, or find more of Noah's heart...

roarandtender.com
Instagram **@roarandtender**
https://roarandtender.substack.com

.